D0572278

The Cat in the Hat's Learning Library

To Mom, with love—T.R.

The editors would like to thank
BARBARA KIEFER, PH.D., Associate Professor of Reading
anf Literature, Teacher's College, Columbia University,
for her assistance in the preparation of this book.

Copyright © Dr. Seuss Enterprises, L.P. 2001
THE CAT IN THE HAT'S LEARNING LIBRARY logos and word mark
are trademarks of Dr. Seuss Enterprises, L.P.
All Rights Reserved
THE CAT IN THE HAT'S LEARNING LIBRARY logo © Dr. Seuss Enterprises, L.P. 1998.

CONDITIONS OF SALE
This book is sold subject to the condition that it shall not, by way of trade or
otherwise, be lent, re-sold, hired out or otherwise circulated without the publisher's
written consent in any form of binding or cover other than that in which it is
published and without a similar condition, including this condition being imposed
on the subsequent purchaser.

14 16 18 20 19 17 15

ISBN: 978-0-00-713061-0

First published by Random House Inc.,
New York, USA
First published in the UK in 2002 by HarperCollins*Children's Books*,
a Division of HarperCollins*Publishers* Ltd
1 London Bridge Street, London SE1 9GF

Visit our website at:
www.harpercollins.co.uk

Printed in India by Replika Press Pvt. Ltd.

Oh, the THINGS you can DO that are GOOD for You!

by Tish Rabe

illustrated by Aristides Ruiz

The Cat in the Hat's Learning Library™

HarperCollins *Children's Books*

I'm the Cat in the Hat
and today is the day,
so jump in, buckle up –
we must leave right away

for the Feeling Great Clinic
in far-off Fadoo.
It's a place part museum,
part circus, part zoo,

where you will soon learn
how to take care of you!
(Your mother will not mind
at all if you do.)

7

Here we are – and the first
friends I'd like you to meet
are two of the famous
Tac-Toe-Tapping Tweet.

Tweet shoot beezerball baskets
by using their feet.

They play every day.
They are strong and they're wise,
for they know to stay healthy
they need exercise!

Exercise gets you going
and helps you to grow.
It gets your heart beating
and makes your blood flow.

What's the Snuff-Gruffle's trouble?
There's no time to play
'cause he sneezes at least
ninety times every day.

When you sneeze, you blow stuff
in a rush from your nose.
(My Sneeze-Meter measures
how far the stuff goes.)

It can travel two metres
and blasts out with great power,
at speeds over well over
150km per hour!

Sneezing shoots germs out
all over the place,
so lift up your arm
and cover your face.

Sneeze into your elbow
so friends won't get sick.

Or sneeze into a tissue –
and throw it out quick!

Germs are small living things
too tiny to see.
Most germs, it is true,
won't hurt you or me.

Now you're in for a treat –
meet the Zing-Singing Zanz.
She has written a song
about washing your hands!

It takes half a minute
to get your hands clean.
Sing along with the Zanz
and you'll see what I mean.

"Wishily washily washily wish.
Squishily squashily squashily squish.

Wash your hands carefully.
It's up to you.
Use soap and warm water.
It's easy to do.

Rinse them and while
we all sing this refrain,

germs from your hands
will slide right down the drain!"

To stay healthy, you need
to keep all of you clean.
So jump into my new
Scrubble-Bubble Machine.

It's part shower, part car wash
and costs just a penny.

It will give you shampoo
(either limey or lemony),
scrub your fingernails free
of the dirt and the grime,
while you finish your homework
all at the same time!

Now please follow me –
you'll be glad that you did
as we tiptoe inside...

Fats

EAT JUST A LITTLE EACH DAY

Milk, Cheese, Yogurt

2-3 SERVINGS PER DAY

Meats, Fish, Poultry, Eggs, Beans, Nuts

2-3 SERVINGS PER DAY

Vegetables

2-4 SERVINGS PER DAY

Fruits

2-4 SERVINGS PER DAY

Bread, Pasta, Rice, Cereal

EAT LOTS EVERY DAY

...the Great Food Pyramid!

Meet the Ee-hip-en-hop,
who are experts at knowing
what foods are the best
for a body that's growing.

They eat –
pasta, rice, cereal,
muffins and breads,
which they munch at small tables
they wear on their heads.

Fruits, vegetables,
lean meats and fish they enjoy
(although some prefer tofu
or milk made from soy).

They like all different foods
but are careful to eat
only morsels of fat
and few things that are sweet.

In the morning, your body
needs food right away.
So be sure to eat breakfast
to start off each day!

In this booth
you'll hear something amazing but true.
You will hear your own body –
it's talking to you!

When you're thirsty, just listen.
Your body says, "Think!
I need to get water –
please drink, drink, drink, drink!"

When you're hungry, your stomach
starts grumbling and mumbling,
"Feed me, or else
I will go right on rumbling!"

When your body feels pain,
it is telling you, "Hey!
Something is wrong.
I need help right away!"

If you start to feel tired,
you can't do your best.
Your body is telling you,
"It's time to rest."

If a voice inside says,
"I feel angry. I'm mad."
Or you hear your heart whisper,
"I feel kind of sad . . ."

...tell a friend how you're feeling –
it's quite okay.
Everyone at some time
gets to feeling that way.

Let me introduce
the Snee Snicker Sneeth!
She is known far and wide
for her sparkling, clean teeth.

Like you, she had baby teeth
when she was small,

but though she grew big,
her teeth grew not at all.

One by one they fell out,
but this smart Snicker Sneeth
knew she had a new set
of teeth growing beneath!

But there's one thing no Sneeth
you will meeth will forget —
this next set of teeth
is the last set you get.

So she brushes her teeth
at least two times a day.
(Germs that stay on your teeth
can lead to decay.)

After brushing your teeth,
take some floss and unwind it.
Then slide it between them.
If food's there – you'll find it!

Keep brushing and flossing –
it's really a breeze
and will help to make sure
you avoid cavities!

Now I'd like you to meet
the Galactic Garoo.
He can juggle six chairs,
five friends and one shoe.

How do Garoo do it?
It's hard to explain,
but it all comes from signals
sent out from the brain.

It's your body's computer
that makes everything go.
Helps you sleep, run and hiccup,
think, dream, smile and grow.

It's important for you to
protect it, and so...

...if you're going out riding
a skateboard or bike,
or doing another fun sport
that you like,

take care to make sure
that your head is all right:
Grab a helmet, and see that
you snap it on tight!

Be smart and be safe,
and just like the Garoo,
make sure that your parents
wear their helmets, too!

Here is where Snug Buggles
tumble and play,
then sleep in a heap
at the end of the day.

Snug Buggles know
the importance of rest.
Ten hours of sleep
helps Buggles do best.

Snug Buggles show us

the way to wake bright –

Go to sleep at about
the same time every night.

Brush your teeth.

Read a book.

Sing a song.

Dim the light.

Take a breath.
Close your eyes.
Just relax…

...and sleep tight.

We all need to sleep.
It's important to do.
But your brain never sleeps.
It keeps working for you.

It keeps your heart beating
inside of your chest
and keeps your lungs breathing
while you get some rest.

Oh, and speaking of sleep,
it is time we must go –
but there's just one more thing
I would like you to know.

You're important and special.
Believe me, it's true!
No one in the world
is exactly like you.

Feeling Great
CLINIC

We learned something together
in far-off Fadoo –
taking care of yourself
is a good thing to do.

GLOSSARY

Cavity: A hole in a tooth caused by decay.

Clinic: A place to get medical treatment.

Decay: To lose strength; to rot.

Energy: The ability to be active.

Exercise: Any activity that promotes physical fitness.

Pyramid: A figure having three or more triangular sides that meet in a point at the top.

Refrain: A part of a song or poem that is repeated.

Tofu: A soft, white food made from soybeans that is high in protein.

INDEX

The Cat in the Hat's Learning Library™

Titles for you to collect:

Fine Feathered Friends

Is a Camel a Mammal?

Oh Say Can You Say DI-NO-SAUR?

**Oh, the Things You Can Do
That Are Good for You!**

On Beyond Bugs!

Wish for a Fish

If you love The Cat in the Hat then look out for these great titles to collect:

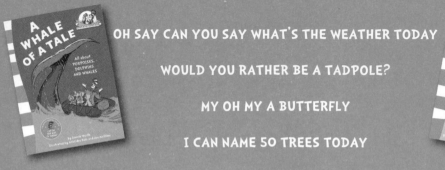

OH SAY CAN YOU SAY WHAT'S THE WEATHER TODAY

WOULD YOU RATHER BE A TADPOLE?

MY OH MY A BUTTERFLY

I CAN NAME 50 TREES TODAY

MILES AND MILES OF REPTILES

A GREAT DAY FOR PUP

CLAM-I-AM!

A WHALE OF A TALE!

THERE'S NO PLACE LIKE SPACE!

OH, THE PETS YOU CAN GET!

IF I RAN THE RAIN FOREST

INSIDE YOUR OUTSIDE!

FINE FEATHERED FRIENDS

OH, THE THINGS YOU CAN DO THAT ARE GOOD FOR YOU!

IS A CAMEL A MAMMAL?

WISH FOR A FISH

OH SAY CAN YOU SAY DI-NO-SAUR?

ON BEYOND BUGS

OH SAY CAN YOU SEED?